D1180791

KEEP YOUR YOUR GIN UP

An exclusive edition for

for all your gift books and gift stationery

This second edition published in 2019
by Allsorted Ltd, Watford, Herts, UK WD19 4BG

Author: Michael Powell
Cover design: Milestone Creative
Contents design: Seagulls

ISBN: 978-1-911517-36-8

Printed in China

KEEP YOUR YOUR GIN UP

WHEN ONLY A SNIFTER WILL DO

GIN

(NOUN): A CLEAR ALCOHOLIC SPIRIT DISTILLED FROM GRAIN OR MALT AND FLAVOURED WITH JUNIPER BERRIES.

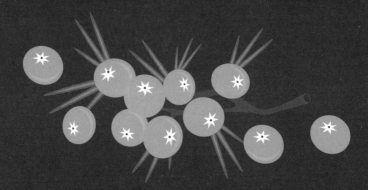

NO JUNIPER, NO GIN

Juniper berries are a vital ingredient in the manufacture of gin. In fact, gin cannot bear the name unless it contains juniper. The name gin is derived from either the Dutch *genever* or French *genièvre*, which both mean juniper. The woody plant is very common, there are about seventy species and they can be easily grown in most countries around the world. All juniper species grow berries (which are not actually berries, but female seed cones), but most are too bitter to eat and some are poisonous.

MEDIEVAL PRECURSOR

The earliest known recipe for a recreational spirit using juniper berries appears in the household book of a rich Dutch merchant who lived between Arnhem and Appledorn in 1495. It uses 10 quarts of wine and heaps of ludicrously expensive spices, which include '12 nutmegs, ginger, galangal, grains of paradise, clove, cinnamon and cardamom'.

GENEVER

The Dutch forerunner of gin, *genever* was manufactured as early as the fifteenth century by distilling malt wine. Distilling techniques were so basic that someone had the idea of adding an abundant local spice – juniper berries – to the unpalatable concoction, and a sophisticated new drink was born.

GIN AND ORANGE

The British have the Dutch king William of Orange to thank for gin. When he arrived in Britain in 1688 he relaxed the laws on making spirits and imposed a heavy duty on all imported spirits such as French brandy. While the upper classes could afford to drink imported Dutch *genever*, the lower classes made their own version and cut it with illicit ingredients such as turpentine and sulfuric acid to give the toxic concoction its warm afterglow. So began the period known as the Gin Craze, which lasted about seventy years.

REJUVENATING JUNIPER

Gin has a rich history of being used for medicinal purposes. Oil from the juniper berry has long been used as a diuretic and to treat indigestion, flatulence and diseases of the kidney and bladder. It's also an effective natural flea repellent. It appears in an Ancient Egyptian papyrus dating to 1550BC as a cure for jaundice. The Ancient Greeks used it to treat colic.

JUNIPER BY JOVE

Roman author, naturalist and natural philosopher, Pliny the Elder, wrote that juniper 'dispels flatulency and sudden chills, soothes cough, and brings indurations to a head'. Topical application 'checks the growth of tumours' and the seed 'is used as a liniment for defluxions of the eyes, and is prescribed for convulsions, ruptures, griping pains in the bowels …'. He also recorded 'there are persons who rub the body with juniper berries as a preventive of the attacks of serpents'.

> **THE FIRST TIME I LOSE I DRINK WHISKEY. SECOND TIME I LOSE I DRINK GIN. THIRD TIME I LOSE I DRINK ANYTHING 'CAUSE I THINK I'M GONNA WIN.**
>
> Gram Parsons

MOTHER'S RUIN

The association between gin and 'mother's ruin' was made famous by the English painter William Hogarth's notorious 1751 etching 'Gin Lane'. It depicts hoards of feckless poverty-stricken gin drinkers and the central figure of a drunk mother dropping her baby. Its contrasting sister print 'Beer Street' shows British ale being drunk by convivial, industrious labourers. The prints were made in support of the Gin Act of the same year which restricted consumption of spirits in an attempt to reduce crime.

MARTINIS SHOULD ALWAYS BE STIRRED, NOT SHAKEN, SO THAT THE MOLECULES LIE SENSUOUSLY ONE ON TOP OF THE OTHER.

W Somerset Maugham

THE THREE-MARTINI LUNCH IS THE EPITOME OF AMERICAN EFFICIENCY. WHERE ELSE CAN YOU GET AN EARFUL, A BELLYFUL AND A SNOOTFUL AT THE SAME TIME?

Gerald R Ford

> I WORK FOR THREE OR FOUR
> HOURS A DAY, IN THE LATE
> MORNING AND EARLY AFTERNOON.
> THEN I GO OUT FOR A WALK AND
> COME BACK IN TIME FOR A LARGE
> GIN AND TONIC.
>
> J G Ballard

GIN TASTING

The best way to taste gins for comparison is at room temperature, diluted with an equal measure of water. This reveals both qualities and flaws.

CLASSIC COCKTAILS

There are more classic cocktails made with gin than any other spirit. This is because distillers can add a range of botanicals that mean that no two brands of gin are alike and they give a cocktail complexity and depth. The most famous gin cocktail is probably Martini, which consists of gin, dry vermouth and optional bitters.

I'VE TRIED BUDDHISM, SCIENTOLOGY, NUMEROLOGY, TRANSCENDENTAL MEDITATION, QABBALA, T'AI CHI, FENG SHUI AND DEEPAK CHOPRA BUT I FIND STRAIGHT GIN WORKS BEST.

Phyllis Diller

YOU'D LEARN MORE ABOUT THE WORLD BY LYING ON THE COUCH AND DRINKING GIN OUT OF A BOTTLE THAN BY WATCHING THE NEWS.

Garrison Keillor

IF YOU'VE HAD GOOD GIN ON A HOT DAY IN SOUTHERN CALIFORNIA WITH THE PEOPLE YOU LOVE, YOU FORGET NEBRASKA. THE TWO THINGS CANNOT COEXIST. THE STRONGER, BETTER OF THE TWO WINS.

Ann Patchett

HOW TO MAKE A GIMLET

Are you too macho to order a gin and lime? Did you know that the Royal Navy used to mix gin with lime cordial to prevent scurvy? The drink became known as the Gimlet.

Ingredients:
75ml gin
37.5ml Rose's Lime Cordial
Lime wheel

Add all the ingredients to a cocktail shaker filled with ice. Shake, strain into a chilled cocktail glass filled with fresh ice and garnish with a lime wheel.

FOR GIN, IN CRUEL SOBER TRUTH, SUPPLIES THE FUEL FOR FLAMING YOUTH.

Noël Coward

THE VESPER

James Bond first ordered his favourite dry martini in the book *Casino Royale* (1953). Actually, it wasn't a martini at all, but his own invention which later became known as a 'Vesper', after the original Bond girl, Vesper Lynd. It consisted of 'Three measures of Gordon's, one of vodka, half a measure of Kina Lillet. Shake it very well until it's ice-cold, then add a large thin slice of lemon peel'.

YOU CAN NO MORE KEEP A MARTINI IN THE REFRIGERATOR THAN YOU CAN KEEP A KISS THERE.

Bernard DeVoto

A REAL GIMLET IS HALF GIN AND HALF ROSE'S LIME JUICE AND NOTHING ELSE.

Raymond Chandler

DUTCH COURAGE

Some say that a Dutch physician named Franciscus Sylvius created the high-proof medicinal spirit *genever* during the seventeenth century, although evidence suggests it was around much earlier. Sylvius used his concoction to improve circulation and to treat a variety of ailments. During the Dutch Independence War, it was issued to soldiers and became known as 'Dutch Courage'.

THE MOST DANGEROUS DRINK IS GIN ... BECAUSE GIN ISN'T REALLY A DRINK, IT'S MORE A MASCARA THINNER.

Dylan Moran

HOW TO MAKE A WHITE LADY

The White Lady is a famous gin-based cocktail, credited to Harry MacElhone in Harry's New York Bar in Paris in 1929 and The Savoy's bartender, Harry Craddock, in 1930.

Ingredients:
40ml gin
30ml triple sec
20ml lemon juice

Pour the ingredients into a cocktail shaker filled with ice. Shake well and strain into a highball glass.

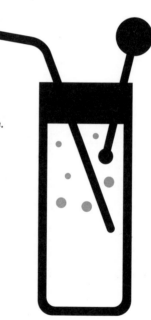

NOTHING MAKES A SOUTHERN STORY BETTER THAN A STRETCH OF TIME AND A FEW GLASSES OF GIN.

M L Bullock

GIN IS A CONFUSING DRINK. IT'S THE ONLY LIQUID THAT'S BOTH WET AND DRY.

Jarod Kintz

LONDON GIN

Although London is widely regarded as the global capital of gin production, London gin does not have to be made in London or even the UK to use the name. However, it must conform to several EU regulations established in February 2008, which include using a neutral base distilled to over 96% ABV, then redistilled to at least 70% ABV; it cannot be watered down beyond 37.5% ABV or contain any artificial ingredients. It can only use minimal sweetener, must be colourless with the predominant flavour of juniper berries and, most important of all, nothing must be added after distillation.

25

GINEBRA SAN MIGUEL

The country with the highest per capita gin consumption in the world is the Philippines, which accounts for over 40% of the global gin market (nearly all of which is the country's local brand, Ginebra San Miguel, which is the best-selling gin in the world). The 80 proof spirit was first produced in 1834 by a family-owned distillery in Manila.

IF IT WASN'T FOR THE OLIVES IN HIS MARTINIS HE'D STARVE TO DEATH.

Milton Berle

WHEN A MAN WHO IS DRINKING NEAT GIN STARTS TALKING ABOUT HIS MOTHER HE IS PAST ALL ARGUMENT.

C S Forester

FORTUNATELY THERE IS GIN, THE SOLE GLIMMER IN THIS DARKNESS. **DO YOU FEEL THE GOLDEN, COPPER-COLOURED LIGHT IT KINDLES IN YOU?** I LIKE WALKING THROUGH THE CITY OF AN EVENING IN THE WARMTH OF GIN.

Albert Camus

GIN SOLO

In 1967, 65-year-old adventurer Sir Francis Chichester became the first man to successfully circumnavigate the world solo in a yacht. It took him nine months and one day and he partially credited his success to a daily glass of pink gin (gin, Angostura bitters and cold water).

A LONELY MAN IS A LONESOME THING, A STONE, A BONE, A STICK, A RECEPTACLE FOR GILBEY'S GIN, A STOOPED FIGURE SITTING AT THE EDGE OF A HOTEL BED, HEAVING COPIOUS SIGHS LIKE THE AUTUMN WIND.

John Cheever

HOW TO MAKE A GIN RICKEY

The Gin Rickey was the most popular gin drink of the late nineteenth and early twentieth centuries.

Ingredients:
60ml gin
7.5ml sugar syrup (2 sugar to 1 water)
1 lime, cut in half
Soda water

Fill a highball glass with ice, add the gin and sugar syrup, squeeze and drop in the lime halves and fill with soda water.

I BOUGHT A PIANO ONCE BECAUSE I HAD THE DREAM OF PLAYING **AS TIME GOES BY** AS SOME GIRL'S LEANING ON IT DRINKING A MARTINI. **GREAT IMAGE.** BUT NONE OF IT WORKED OUT. I CAN'T EVEN PLAY CHOPSTICKS. **BUT I'VE GOT A NICE PIANO AT MY HOUSE!**

George Clooney

NOW ALL THE CRIMINALS IN THEIR SUITS AND TIES ARE FREE TO DRINK MARTINIS AND WATCH THE SUNRISE.

Bob Dylan

LOVE DRINKING GIN AND TONIC?

—

You could be a psychopath, research suggests. Two experiments conducted on 1,000 people by Innsbruck University in Austria found that people with psychopathic tendencies are more likely to prefer bitter foods and drinks.

|||||||||||||||||||||||||||||||||||||||||||||||||||||||||||||||||||||||||||||||||||||||||||||||||||||||

HOW TO MAKE A SINGAPORE SLING

The Singapore Sling is a gin-based cocktail, developed in the early twentieth century in Raffles Hotel, Singapore. It appeared in 1930 in the *Savoy Cocktail Book* as '¼ lemon juice, ¼ Dry Gin, ½ Cherry Brandy: shake well and strain into medium size glass, and fill with soda water. Add one lump of ice'. Today the International Bartenders Association (IBA) ingredients are:

30ml gin
15ml cherry liqueur (cherry brandy)
7.5ml Cointreau
7.5ml DOM Bénédictine
10ml grenadine
120ml pineapple juice
15ml fresh lime juice
1 dash Angostura bitters

Pour the ingredients into a cocktail shaker filled with ice. Shake well, strain into a highball glass and garnish with pineapple and a cocktail cherry.

ONE MARTINI IS JUST RIGHT, TWO IS TOO MANY, THREE IS NOT ENOUGH.

35

||||||||||||||||||||||||||||||||||||||||||||||||||||||||||||||||||||||||||||||||||||||||||||||||||||||

SHAKEN AND NOT STIRRED

James Bond didn't utter the famous instruction 'shaken and not stirred' until *Dr. No* (1958). Many bartenders disagree, and would recommend a stirred martini instead, as shaking dilutes the drink too much.

I HAVE EITHER A CUCUMBER MARTINI, GIN MARTINI, OR A VODKA MARTINI. THAT'S IT. SIMPLE.

Robert De Niro

MOONSHOT GIN

In 2017, the newly formed That Boutique-y Gin Company launched its flagship product: Moonshot Gin. Its botanicals include juniper, coriander, cubeb pepper, fresh lemon peel, camomile flowers, cardamom, dried bitter orange peel, cinnamon, liquorice root and angelica. They all have an added attraction – they have been sent into the stratosphere to an altitude of at least 20km where they were 'exposed to extremely low pressures'. Each bottle also contains a tiny fragment of moon rock from a lunar meteorite.

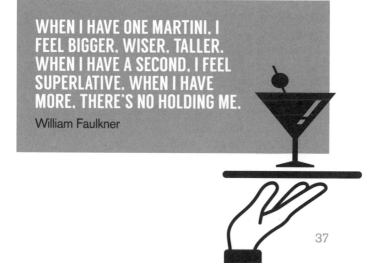

WHEN I HAVE ONE MARTINI, I FEEL BIGGER, WISER, TALLER. WHEN I HAVE A SECOND, I FEEL SUPERLATIVE. WHEN I HAVE MORE, THERE'S NO HOLDING ME.

William Faulkner

LEMONS FROM GEORGIA

At the Yalta Conference in February 1945, President Roosevelt complained that there were no lemons to make twists for the martinis. Stalin had a lemon tree flown in from Georgia the same day.

THE GIN CRAZE

In 1621, there were 200 registered distillers in London. In 1690, Parliament passed 'An Act for encouraging the distilling of brandy and spirits from corn' to make use of a corn surplus. The result was an explosion of amateur distilling. Consumption of spirits rose from 2,600,363 litres (572,000 gallons) in 1684 to 5,455,308 litres (1.2 million gallons) in 1700. By 1730, gin consumption alone reached 13,638,276 litres (3 million gallons) and this rose to a peak of 36 million litres (8 million gallons) by 1742 – about two gallons per capita – nearly all of it unlicensed.

I BELIEVE IN RED MEAT. I'VE OFTEN SAID: RED MEAT AND GIN.

Julia Child

39

MEDITATING DEEPLY SO THAT SHE COULD REALLY, CLEARLY EXPERIENCE BEING **ANGRY AND LONESOME AND HURT AND HORROR-STRUCK** NEVER SEEMED AS GOOD AS A **STRONG GIN AND TONIC** AND ANOTHER HOUR OF WORK.

James S A Corey

HOW TO MAKE A HOT GIN TWIST

Gin hasn't always been drunk ice-cold. London's most popular drink in the winter of 1823 was the Hot Gin Twist consisting of hot water and gin, with sugar and lemon juice. It was so popular that it inspired a 145-line poem by William Maginn, 'A Twist-imony in favour of Gin-twist', which began:

At one in the morn, as I went staggering home,
With nothing at all in my hand but my fist,
At the end of the street a good youth I did meet,
Who asked me to join in a jug of gin-twist.
'Though 'tis late,' I replied, 'and I'm muggy beside,
Yet an offer like this I could never resist;
So let's waddle away, sans a moment's delay,
And in style we'll demolish your jug of gin-twist!'

Ingredients:
40ml gin
25ml fresh lemon juice (juice of half a lemon)
1 heaped tablespoonful of sugar, to taste
120-150ml boiling water

Combine the ingredients in a teacup, mug or Irish coffee mug. Stir. Garnish with a lemon twist.

IF A WOMAN ACCUSTOMS
HERSELF TO DRAM-DRINKING
SHE ... BECOMES THE MOST
MISERABLE AS WELL AS
THE MOST CONTEMPTIBLE
CREATURE ON EARTH.

Anon, 'A dissertation on Mr Hogarth's Six Prints', 1751

HOW TO MAKE
A HANKY-PANKY

This elegant cocktail was created specially for the debonair actor-manager Sir Charles Henry Hawtrey by Ada Coleman (known as Coley), a bartender at London's Savoy Hotel. She told the story behind its creation to England's *The People* newspaper in 1925:

> The late Charles Hawtrey ... was one of the best judges of cocktails that I knew. Some years ago, when he was overworking, he used to come into the bar and say, 'Coley, I am tired. Give me something with a bit of punch in it!' It was for him that I spent hours

experimenting until I had invented a new cocktail. The next time he came in, I told him I had a new drink for him. He sipped it, and, draining the glass, he said, 'By Jove! That is the real hanky-panky!' And Hanky-Panky it has been called ever since.

Ingredients:
50ml gin
50ml sweet vermouth
5ml Fernet-Branca (a bitter Italian digestivo)
10ml freshly squeezed orange juice
Orange twist

Add all the ingredients to a mixing glass and fill with ice. Stir, and strain into a chilled cocktail glass and garnish with an orange twist.

IT'S TOO WARM FOR RED WINE;
NOW I MIX GIN AND TONICS
INSTEAD. I FIND THEY MAKE THE
ORDINARY SENSATION OF LIVING
LIGHTER, LESS RUFFLED.

Sara Baume

A NEW KIND OF DRUNKENNESS IS LATELY SPRUNG UP AMONGST US – WHICH – IF NOT PUT A STOP TO, WILL INFALLIBLY DESTROY A GREAT PART OF THE INFERIOR PEOPLE … THE INTOXICATING DRAUGHT ITSELF DISQUALIFIES THEM FROM USING ANY HONEST MEANS TO ACQUIRE IT, AT THE SAME TIME IT REMOVES ALL SENSE OF FEAR AND SHAME AND EMBOLDENS THEM TO COMMIT EVERY WICKED AND DESPERATE ENTERPRISE … WHAT MUST BECOME OF THE INFANT WHO IS CONCEIVED IN GIN? WITH THE POISONOUS DISTILLATIONS OF WHICH IT IS NOURISHED BOTH IN THE WOMB AND AT THE BREAST.

Henry Fielding, 'Enquiry into the Causes of the late Increase of Robbers etc. with some proposals for remedying this growing evil', 1751

I'M HAVING A LOTTALITTLE.

LOTTA GIN, LITTLE BIT OF TONIC.

Jennifer Skutelsky

45

THE DRINKING OF GIN AT ONE TIME THREATENED, LITERALLY, TO DESTROY THE WHOLE OF THE WORKING CLASSES OF LONDON.

Walter Besant, *The History of London*

> MY MAIN AMBITION AS A GARDENER IS TO WATER MY ORANGE TREES WITH GIN. THEN ALL I HAVE TO DO IS SQUEEZE THE JUICE INTO A GLASS.
>
> W C Fields

OLD TOM

During the eighteenth century Gin Craze, in order to make cheap gin more palatable, distillers sweetened it with liquorice or sugar, thus creating a whole new type of gin, colloquially known as Old Tom. It is often described as the missing link between the flavours of Dutch *genever* and London dry gin.

> NEVER DRINK WHEN YOU ARE WRETCHED WITHOUT IT. OR YOU WILL BE LIKE THE GREY-FACED GIN-DRINKER IN THE SLUM; BUT DRINK WHEN YOU WOULD BE HAPPY WITHOUT IT. AND YOU WILL BE LIKE THE LAUGHING PEASANT OF ITALY.
>
> G K Chesterton

PUSS AND MEW

The world's first drinks vending machines dispensed gin. The name Old Tom became associated with the Puss and Mew slot machines that popped up around London to sell gin for two pence a shot. Gin sellers would advertise with wooden signs with a black cat on their outside walls and customers would deposit money in a slot and say, 'Puss, give me two pennyworth of gin'. The supplier would respond, 'Mew', and pour a measure of gin through a tube which ended underneath the cat's paw. The customer would either drink it immediately or collect it in a cup or flask.

WHEN HE BUYS HIS TIES HE HAS TO ASK IF GIN WILL MAKE THEM RUN.

F Scott Fitzgerald

HIS TWO GREAT LOVES WERE HARD WORK AND HARD WORK'S REWARD — WHISKEY, WHEN HE COULD GET IT, AND GIN WHEN HE COULD NOT.

Eleanor Catton

CAT AND BARREL

Old Tom Gin has always been associated with a cat logo. In fact, gin distillers fought over the right to stick a cat on their product. In 1849, Joseph Boord of London became the first manufacturer of Old Tom to register a Cat and Barrel trademark. In the winter of 1903, Boord & Sons won a landmark court case defending their trademark against Huddart & Company under 'passing-off laws'.

BY 12.30, GILES HAD CONSUMED FIVE GIN-RICKIES, FOUR GIN-AND-TONICS, THREE GIN-AND-ITS, TWO GIN-AND-BITTERS, AND ONE GIN.

Martin Amis

II

HOW TO MAKE A BEE'S KNEES

—

The Bee's Knees was the bee's knees during the Roaring Twenties.

Ingredients:
60ml gin
22.5ml fresh lemon juice
3 spoons runny honey
Lemon twist

Add all the ingredients to a cocktail shaker and fill with ice. Strain into a small chilled cocktail glass and serve with a lemon twist.

NO MAN IS GENUINELY HAPPY, MARRIED, WHO HAS TO DRINK WORSE GIN THAN HE USED TO DRINK WHEN HE WAS SINGLE.

H L Mencken

GIN AND BEAR IT

In 1751, the Gin Act was the first nail in the coffin for mass gin drinking in Britain. The poor grain harvests between 1757 and 1763 then put many small distillers out of business. As gin became more expensive to make, so the price and quality rose. Mother's Ruin was soon too expensive for mass consumption and became a rich person's drink.

THERE'S TRUTH IN WINE, AND THERE MAY BE SOME IN GIN AND MUDDY BEER; BUT WHETHER IT'S TRUTH WORTH MY KNOWING, IS ANOTHER QUESTION.

George Eliot

GORDON'S

Gordon's London Dry Gin was first distilled in 1769 by Alexander Gordon in Bermondsey, south London. Today Gordon's Gin is made in Fife, Scotland, and remains Britain's top-selling gin. The botanicals are a trade secret, but they are believed to include juniper, coriander seeds, angelica root, liquorice root, orris root, orange peel and lemon peel.

THE SHORTEST WAY OUT OF MANCHESTER IS NOTORIOUSLY A BOTTLE OF GORDON'S GIN.

William Bolitho

HOW TO MAKE AN AVIATION

This classic violet-coloured cocktail was invented before Prohibition.

Ingredients:
52.5ml gin
7.5ml crème de violette or Crème Yvette
15ml maraschino liqueur
15ml lemon juice

Add the ingredients into a cocktail shaker filled with ice. Shake well, strain into a cocktail glass and garnish with a cherry.

BOMBAY SAPPHIRE

The recent revival in the popularity of gin is thanks to one brand, launched in 1987 by International Distillers and Vintners. Bombay Sapphire has a light, floral taste and has ten botanicals: juniper, almond, angelica root, cassia bark, coriander seeds, cubeb berries, grains of paradise, lemon peel, liquorice root and orris root.

I EXERCISE SELF CONTROL. I NEVER DRINK ANYTHING STRONGER THAN GIN BEFORE BREAKFAST.

W C Fields

THE PROPER UNION OF GIN AND VERMOUTH IS A GREAT AND SUDDEN GLORY; IT IS ONE OF THE HAPPIEST MARRIAGES ON EARTH AND ONE OF THE SHORTEST LIVED.

Bernard DeVoto

THAT HUMBLE AND MUCH REVILED LIQUID WHICH IS THE MOST ESPECIALLY ENGLISH OF ALL SPIRITS.

William Henry Hazlitt

LAVERSTOCK MILL

In 2014, production of Bombay Sapphire moved to Laverstock Mill in Hampshire, England. This included the restoration of a former paper mill and the erection of two extraordinary glasshouses, works of art in themselves designed by Thomas Heatherwick, for growing the botanicals, as well as an award-winning visitor centre.

ZEN MARTINI: A MARTINI WITH NO VERMOUTH AT ALL. AND NO GIN, EITHER.

P J O'Rourke

THE ONLY TIME I EVER ENJOYED IRONING WAS THE DAY I ACCIDENTALLY GOT GIN IN THE STEAM IRON.

Phyllis Diller

PLYMOUTH GIN

Plymouth Gin has been manufactured in Black Friars distillery in Plymouth, England, since 1793. The ship on the bottle is *The Mayflower*, based on the local belief that the Pilgrim Fathers had to put into Plymouth for repairs and some of them stayed at the site (which in 1620 was a Dominican Order monastery). Its 160-year-old still continues to be used today, and is reported to be the oldest gin distillery still producing gin.

BRIGHT WAS THE LIGHT OF MY LAST MARTINI ON MY MORAL HORIZON.

Norman Mailer

SWEETER AND FRUITIER

Plymouth Gin was the official gin of the British Royal Navy. During the middle of the nineteenth century, Coates and Co was supplying the Navy with over 1,000 casks a year. Plymouth Gin is sweeter and fruitier than a basic London Gin and has seven botanicals: juniper, coriander seed, orange peel, lemon peel, green cardamom, angelica root and orris root.

THIS IS AN EXCELLENT MARTINI – SORT OF TASTES LIKE IT ISN'T THERE AT ALL, JUST A COLD CLOUD.

Herman Wouk

HOW TO MAKE A MONKEY GLAND

The Monkey Gland cocktail was created in the 1920s by Harry MacElhone, owner of Harry's New York Bar in Paris, France.

Ingredients:
60ml gin
45ml orange juice
3.8ml grenadine
Dash of absinthe
Orange slice garnis

Swirl a dash of absinthe in a chilled cocktail glass to coat it, then pour away any excess liqueur. Pour the remaining ingredients into a cocktail shaker with ice cubes. Shake well, strain into the cocktail glass and garnish with an orange slice.

WHEN A HORSE LEARNS TO BUY MARTINIS, I'LL LEARN TO LIKE HORSES.

Steve McQueen

MURIEL'S CAFE BAR

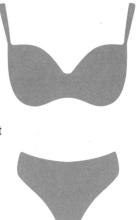

Situated in Belfast, Northern Ireland, Muriel's Café Bar stocks more than 130 gins. If you join its Juniper Club you will receive a special passport that takes you 'around the world in eighty gins'. Choose one of the colourful luggage tags that fills a vintage suitcase and enjoy a gin from that country plus a recommended cocktail. Bras and pants hang above the bar on the first floor in tribute to Muriel, who ran a hat shop on the ground floor by day and a brothel at night.

MARTINIS ARE THE ONLY AMERICAN INVENTION AS PERFECT AS A SONNET.

H L Mencken

TANQUERAY

In 1830, Charles Tanqueray distilled his gin for the first time in the Bloomsbury area of London, then famed for its waters. Production continued on the site until its almost total destruction during the Second World War. The recipe is a closely guarded secret, but the key botanicals are known to be juniper, coriander, angelica root and liquorice. Today Tanqueray London Dry Gin is manufactured at Cameron Bridge, Scotland, and is the highest selling imported gin in the United States.

A MAN MUST DEFEND HIS HOME. HIS WIFE. HIS CHILDREN. AND HIS MARTINI.

Jackie Gleason

TONY SINCLAIR

The eccentric character Tony Sinclair appears in Tanqueray adverts with his catchphrase 'Ready to Tanqueray?' followed by his manic laugh. He was devised and played by California-based actor, rapper, dancer and stand-up comedian Rodney Mason who is five foot six inches tall and describes himself as 'physically fit and very athletic'.

HAPPINESS IS FINDING TWO OLIVES IN YOUR MARTINI WHEN YOU'RE HUNGRY.

Johnny Carson

HOW TO MAKE A TOM COLLINS

The first written record of the Tom Collins appeared in the 1876 edition of the *Bar-Tender's Guide* by 'Professor' Jerry Thomas, the father of American mixology.

Ingredients:
15ml simple syrup
30ml lemon juice
60ml Old Tom gin
Soda water
Lemon slice

Fill a collins glass with ice. Add all the ingredients to the glass and top with a splash of soda water. Garnish with a slice of lemon.

GIN AND CHEESE, SHE THOUGHT AS SHE REFILLED HER DRINK. ALL THE NECESSARY FOOD GROUPS FOR A MELANCHOLY WOMAN.

Tess Gerritsen

||||||||||||||||||||||||||||||||||||||||||||||||||||||||||||||||||||||||||||||||||||||||

LOCH NESS GIN

The House of Elrick has been making its handcrafted artisan gin in the lowlands of Aberdeenshire since 1720, at the height of the Scottish Enlightenment. It uses fresh water from Loch Ness and produces only 600 bottles per run. It describes the taste profile as 'a fresh, yet earthy, bold infusion of flavours'. The key botanicals include juniper, coriander seeds, angelica root and citrus peel, built around a core of heather, pink peppercorns, sweet fennel and rose petals. The estate was once visited by Bonnie Prince Charlie, who gifted the Jacobite Rose which still grows today in its beautiful walled garden.

I LIKE TO HAVE A MARTINI, TWO
AT THE VERY MOST; THREE, I'M
UNDER THE TABLE, FOUR I'M
UNDER MY HOST!

Dorothy Parker

GIN AHOY!

Gin and tonic was popularised throughout colonial India because the tonic contained quinine, used as a malaria treatment. Today, most commercial tonic waters contain much smaller amounts of quinine than previously, so you'd have to drink several litres to experience ill effects such as ringing in the ears, rashes, itching or blurred vision. However, some people are hypersensitive to the drug, so if you experience any of these symptoms, avoid tonic water altogether. The late English chef and former barrister Clarissa Dickson Wright, best known as one of television's *Two Fat Ladies*, claimed to have irreparably damaged her adrenal gland by drinking too many gin and tonics.

I NEVER GO JOGGING, IT MAKES ME SPILL MY MARTINI.

George Burns

HOW TO MAKE A NEGRONI

Legend has it that this favourite bitter aperitif was invented in Florence in 1919 when Count Negroni asked for gin in place of the soda in his Americano (Campari, vermouth and soda).

Ingredients:
45ml Campari
45ml gin
45ml sweet vermouth
Orange half-wheel garnish

Add all the ingredients to a chilled cocktail glass filled with ice. Stir until cold and garnish with an orange half-wheel.

LIQUID MADNESS SOLD AT TENPENCE THE QUARTERN.

Thomas Carlyle

GIN BLOSSOMS

The burst capillaries at the end of the noses of many heavy drinkers are colloquially referred to as 'gin blossoms'. Gin Blossoms is also the name of an American rock band formed in 1987 in Tempe, Arizona, best known for the song 'Hey Jealousy' from their four-times platinum album, *New Miserable Experience* (1992).

THE GIN AND TONIC HAS SAVED MORE ENGLISHMEN'S LIVES AND MINDS, THAN ALL THE DOCTORS IN THE EMPIRE.

Winston Churchill

CHURCHILL MARTINI

Legend has it that Winston Churchill made his martinis by pouring a glass of Plymouth gin, then glancing at a bottle of vermouth from the other side of the room, which is why neat gin is often referred to as a 'Churchill Martini.'

A PERFECT MARTINI SHOULD BE MADE BY FILLING A GLASS WITH GIN THEN WAVING IT IN THE GENERAL DIRECTION OF ITALY.

Noël Coward

I'M EMBARRASSED TO RECEIVE YOU LYING DOWN. IT'S NOTHING: A SLIGHT TEMPERATURE THAT I'M TREATING WITH GIN.

Albert Camus

HOW TO MAKE A HONOLULU

The Honolulu cocktail was one of the signature cocktails in 1930's Hollywood.

Ingredients:
60ml gin
7.5ml pineapple juice
7.5ml fresh orange juice
7.5ml lemon juice
7.5ml simple syrup
1 dash Angostura bitters

Pour the ingredients into a cocktail shaker with ice cubes. Shake well and strain into a sugar-rimmed cocktail glass and garnish with a twist of lemon peel.

> IN WESTERN AUSTRALIA THEY DON'T EVEN KNOW HOW TO MAKE THAT VITAL PIECE OF SAILBOATING EQUIPMENT. THE GIN AND TONIC.
>
> P J O'Rourke

THE WORLD'S MOST EXPENSIVE GIN

Watenshi costs £2,000 for a 70cl bottle. Only six bottles have been made (sold exclusively through Selfridges in London) because it took 100 distillations to make each one. At each distillation, its British creator, Will Lowe, used a 'trap' chilled to minus 75 degrees Celsius (minus 103 degrees Fahrenheit) to capture just the 'angel's share' – the tiny amount normally lost to evaporation during distilling (Watenshi means 'angel's share'). He claims there is nothing else on the market that can compete with the resulting intensity and complexity of his premium Japanese gin. Its key botanicals include juniper, yuzu peel, shiso leaf, sansho pepper, sesame seeds and cucumber.

GIN FOR EXECUTIONS, BEER FOR BIRTHDAYS, WINE FOR WEDDINGS.

P J Wolfson

81

NOLET'S RESERVE

Located in Scheidam in the Netherlands, the Nolet Distillery is considered one of the world's finest. One of the rarest and most expensive gins in the world, at around £450 for a 75cl bottle, Nolet's Reserve Dry Gin is 52.3% and is intended to be sipped to fully enjoy its unprecedented complexity and balance. The handcrafted recipe highlights two distinctive botanicals: warm spicy saffron and subtle, delicate citrus verbena.

> LIKE A GREAT FOOL, I WENT ASHORE WITH THEM, AND THEY GAVE ME SOME CURSED STUFF THEY CALLED GIN – SUCH BLASPHEMY I NEVER HEARD ... THIS WAS THE UNCHRISTIANEST BEASTLIEST LIQUOR I EVER TASTED.
>
> Edward John Trelawny

GIN & JUICE

Gin is the most rapped-about spirit. From Snoop Dogg's 'Gin & Juice' to Wiz Khalifa's 'O.N.I.F.C.' ("Drinking Bombay so I'm slizzered"), gin has consistently surpassed Cristal, rum, vodka, whisky and tequila for the frequency of its appearance in rapper lyrics. Tanqueray is famously the top tipple of choice for Snoop, Dr Dre, and DJ Quik to accompany their beloved 'blunts'.

GIVE ME A PAPER AND PEN, SO I CAN WRITE ABOUT MY LIFE OF SIN. A COUPLE OF BOTTLES OF GIN, IN CASE I DON'T GET IN.

Tupac Shakur

HOW TO MAKE A SOUTHSIDE COCKTAIL

This classy summer drink is like a Mojito in which the rum is replaced by gin. Top up with soda water to make a Southside Fizz, or with champagne to make a Southside Royale.

Ingredients:
8 mint leaves
60ml gin
30ml fresh lime juice
15ml sugar syrup

Pour the ingredients into a cocktail shaker with plenty of ice cubes. Shake well and strain into a chilled martini glass and garnish with a mint leaf.

MARTINI ON THE ROCK

If you want to propose marriage and you have US$10,000 to spend on a diamond, you can visit the Algonquin Hotel in midtown Manhattan, New York City, and order 'Martini on the Rock'. The drink is carefully prepared with a 1.5 carat cut diamond at the bottom of the glass. You must give advance notice of 72 hours so that you can personally select the diamond from the vaults of the hotel's in-house jeweller.

IF PLATO
IS A FINE
RED WINE,
THEN
ARISTOTLE
IS A DRY
MARTINI.

Eric Stoltz

THERE IS SOMETHING ABOUT GIN, THE TANG IN IT OF THE DEEP WILDWOOD, PERHAPS, THAT ALWAYS MAKES ME THINK OF TWILIGHT AND MISTS AND DEAD MAIDENS.

John Banville

THERE'S TOO MUCH LIME IN THE WORLD AND NOT ENOUGH GIN.

Frank O'Hara

88

THE GINSTITUTE

If you have £100 to blow on an experience to create your own bespoke bottle of gin, look no further than The Ginstitute (The Portobello Star, 171 Portobello Road, Notting Hill, London, W11 2DY). You'll be guided around a recreation of a Victorian gin palace with lots of gin-related artefacts; then you get a tutored tasting in The Still Room, where you can choose the blend of botanicals to make your own bottle of Portobello Road No. 171 gin to take home.

ALL MY LIFE I'VE BEEN TERRIBLE AT REMEMBERING PEOPLE'S NAMES. I ONCE INTRODUCED A FRIEND OF MINE AS MARTINI. HER NAME WAS ACTUALLY OLIVE.

Tallulah Bankhead

DUKES BAR

Dukes Bar (St James' Place, London, SW1A 1NY) was a regular watering hole of James Bond author Ian Fleming. He is reputed to have come up with the famous line 'shaken, not stirred' during one of his visits to this exclusive Mayfair establishment, famous for making one of the best martinis in the world. Its website boasts: 'Alessandro Palazzi has created "89 Jermyn Street", a new martini created in partnership with London-based perfumery Floris, whose "89" Eau de Cologne was famously worn by James Bond. The flavour and smoothness of this martini is a sophisticated complement to the aroma of this quintessentially English gentleman's fragrance.'

NO, JOY, YOU JUST THINK GIN MAKES YOU BRILLIANT. GIN MAKES YOU SOTTED. CHOCOLATE MAKES YOU BRILLIANT.

Katie MacAlister

I SMELLED OF GIN. NOT JUST CASUALLY, AS IF I HAD TAKEN FOUR OR FIVE DRINKS OF A WINTER MORNING TO GET OUT OF BED ON, BUT AS IF THE PACIFIC OCEAN WAS PURE GIN AND I HAD NOSEDIVED OFF THE BOAT DECK.

Raymond Chandler

||||||||||||||||||||||||||||||||||||||||||||||||||||||||||||||||||||||||||||||||||||||||||||||||||||||||||||

SIPSMITH TOURS

If you want to learn more about how gin is made, take a tour of the Sipsmith distillery (83 Cranbrook Road, Chiswick, London, W4 2LJ), the first gin distillery to open in London since 1820. For £25 you'll be greeted with a complementary gin and tonic before being introduced to their 'three copper ladies, Prudence, Patience and Constance'. Learn how their award-winning spirits are carefully handcrafted and then enjoy a tutored tasting session. If you've got more cash to splash, you can spend £85 to end your tour with 'a 10 minute walk to one of Chiswick's finest restaurants, Charlotte's Bistro, where you will continue your gin-filled evening with a delicious gin inspired three course supper'. You'll also get your own 35cl bottle of Sipsmith London Dry Gin to take home.

||||||||||||||||||||||||||||||||||||||||||||||||||||||||||||||||||||||||||||||||||||||||||||||

HOW TO MAKE A RED SNAPPER

The Red Snapper is gin's reply to the vodka-based Bloody Mary and it can work just as well for a hair of the dog mid-morning shot in the arm. It's a relative newcomer: although there was a vodka-based version of the Red Snapper in Crosby Gaige's *Cocktail Guide and Ladies Companion* in 1941, the gin version first appeared in *The London Magazine* in 1962.

Ingredients:
30ml gin
120ml tomato juice
15ml lemon juice
7 drops Tabasco hot sauce
4 dashes Worcestershire sauce
2 pinches celery salt
2 grinds black pepper

Pour the ingredients into a cocktail shaker with ice cubes. Shake well and strain into a salt and pepper rimmed collins glass and garnish with half a celery stick.

MOST PEOPLE HAVE SOME MEANS OF FILLING UP THE GAP BETWEEN PERCEPTION AND REALITY. AND, AFTER ALL, IN THOSE CIRCUMSTANCES THERE ARE FAR WORSE THINGS THAN GIN.

Terry Pratchett

GIN-DRINKING IS A GREAT VICE IN ENGLAND, BUT WRETCHEDNESS AND DIRT ARE A GREATER; AND UNTIL YOU IMPROVE THE HOMES OF THE POOR, OR PERSUADE A HALF-FAMISHED WRETCH NOT TO SEEK RELIEF IN THE TEMPORARY OBLIVION OF HIS OWN MISERY, WITH THE PITTANCE, WHICH DIVIDED AMONG HIS FAMILY WOULD FURNISH A MORSEL OF BREAD FOR EACH, GIN-SHOPS WILL INCREASE IN NUMBER AND SPLENDOUR.

Charles Dickens, *Sketches By Boz*, 1836

I HAVE THREE RULES TO LIVE BY: GET YOUR WORK DONE. IF THAT DOESN'T WORK, SHUT UP AND DRINK YOUR GIN, AND WHEN ALL ELSE FAILS, RUN LIKE HELL.

Ray Bradbury